ADDING

DISCARD

Author
Karen Bryant-Mole

Starting Maths

Numbers
Shapes
Weight
Adding
Measuring
Taking Away

Series Editor: Deborah Elliott

First published in 1990 by
Wayland (Publishers) Limited
61 Western Road, Hove
East Sussex, BN3 1JD, England

© Copyright 1990 Wayland (Publishers) Limited

British Library Cataloguing in Publication Data
Bryant-Mole, Karen
  Adding
  1. Arithmetic. Addition
  I. Title II. Series
  513.2

ISBN 1 85210 875 4

Typeset by Nicola Taylor, Wayland
Printed by Rotolito, Italy.
Bound by Casterman S.A., Belgium.

All the words that appear in **bold** are explained in the glossary on page 30.

Contents

Do you know your numbers? 4
Can you put numbers in the right order? 6
Is it 'more' or 'less'? 8
Can you add on 1? 10
Can you add two groups together? 12
Can you write a sum? 14
Can you write these sums? 16
Can you be a magician? 18
Can you find different ways to make 10? 20
Can you count up to 20? 22
Can you add up to 20? 24
Can you add more than two numbers together? 26
Can you work out what the sum should be? 28
Glossary 30
Books To Read 31
Index 32

Do you know your numbers?

Helene has been for a walk in the country. She has collected lots of interesting things and has sorted them into different groups. She has counted up how many objects are in each group and has written the number on some labels.

How many leaves has Helene collected?
How many stones did she find?
How many feathers are there?

The labels for these fruits are waiting to be sorted out. Can you work out which label goes with which fruit?

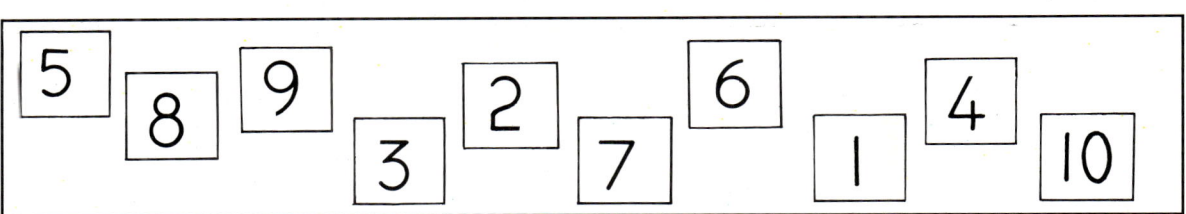

Can you put numbers in the right order?

When we count from 1 to 10 we always say the numbers in the same order.

Can you read the numbers in the pictures opposite? Start at 1 and read each number up to 10.

Here are 10 hotel keys. They each have a **tag** showing a room number.
Some have just been handed in and are waiting to be hung up.
Can you work out where each key should go?

Is it 'more' or 'less'?

Karen and Luke want to know whether the number of marbles is more than or less than the number of cars.

They count them up.
There are 5 cars and 7 marbles.
Are there more marbles or more cars?

To make sure, Karen and Luke match up the cars and marbles side by side.

Yes. There are more marbles than cars.

Can you add on 1?

Helene and Joss are decorating their Christmas tree.

Helene is holding a shiny bell.

How many shiny bells are hanging on the tree?

How many will there be when Helene has hung up her bell?

Here is a nest with 5 eggs.

Which of these pictures shows what the nest would be like if 1 more egg is added?

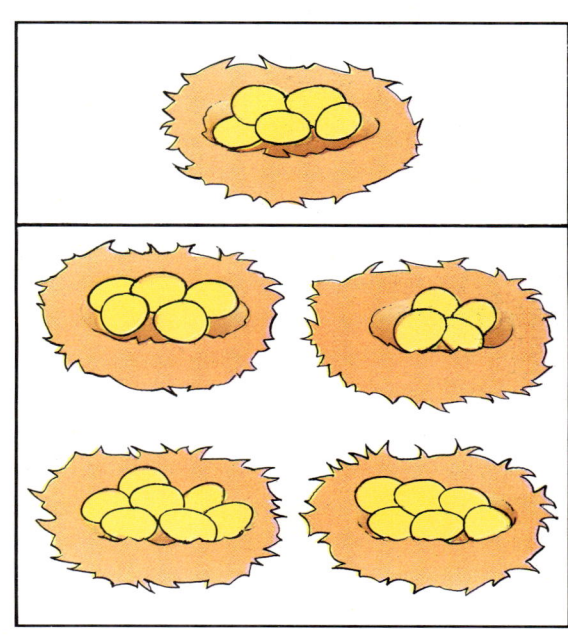

Can you add two groups together?

12

Anne is counting the number of shells in her collection.

How many round shells has she got?
How many long shells has she got?

To find out how many shells Anne has altogether, add the number of round shells and the number of long shells together.
How many shells are there altogether?

Here are some flowers to count.

Count up the number of flowers in each group.
How many would there be if the two groups were added together?

13

Can you write a sum?

Melanie and Edward are at the library.

How many books has Melanie chosen?
How many books has Edward chosen?

Instead of writing, Melanie has 4 books and Edward has 3 books so together they have 7 books, we could write a sum.
To write a sum we need to use **symbols** as well as numbers.

This symbol: + means 'add'.
This symbol: – means 'makes' or 'equals'.

The sum that tells the story of Melanie and Edward's book is
4 + 3 = 7

Work out the sum that tells this story.

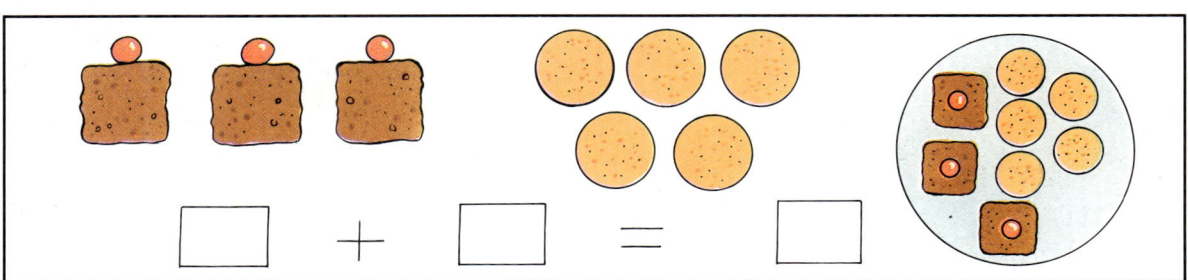

15

Can you write these sums?

Laura's dad is in charge of the cake **stall** at the fair. He has 6 cakes on his stall. Karen brings him 2 more.

How many cakes are there now?
The sum for this story is 6 + 2 = 8.

Here are some other stalls that you might see at a fair.
Can you work out a sum for each stall?

Here are four sums.
One does not tell the story of a stall.
Which one is it?

2 + 3 = 5   4 + 5 = 9
   3 + 5 = 8   4 + 2 = 6

Can you be a magician?

Did you know that you can do magic tricks with adding up sums?

Add up the numbers on one of the cards.
Add up the numbers on the other card.
The answer is the same.
Did you notice that the numbers are the same but in a different order?

Try it for yourself.
2 + 6 will give you the same answer as 6 + 2.
7 + 3 will give you the same answer as 3 + 7.

Have a go at this puzzle.

The clown with the red hat has got sums with answers on his balloons. Use these balloons to work out the answers to the sums on the other clown's balloons.

Can you find different ways to make ten?

Jane has invited 5 girls and 4 boys to her party.

How many people has she invited altogether?
If you include Jane too, how many children will be at the party?

Here are the party things that Jane's mum has bought.
There are 10 of each.

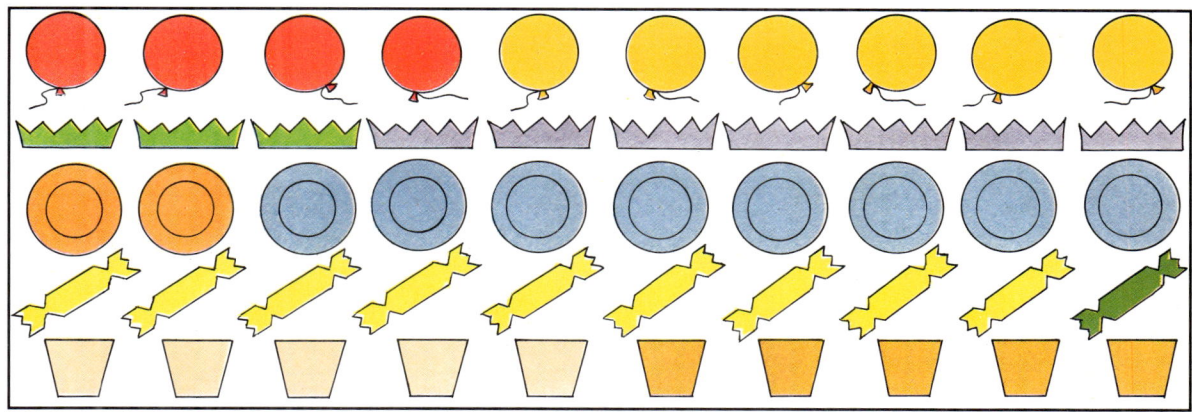

See how many of each colour there are and work out which pairs of numbers add up to 10.

Can you write the sums?
Here is the sum for the balloons
4 + 6 = 10.

21

Can you count to 20?

22

How many glasses of squash can you see?
How many straws are there?

Is the number of straws more than or less than the number of glasses?

Some of these racing cars have lost their numbers.
Here are the numbers that have fallen off.
Which cars do they belong to?

| 12 | 15 | 17 | 20 |

Can you add up to 20?

Ben and Annabel collect stamps. They are sorting them out into different countries so that they can put them in their new stamp albums.

Ben has 9 Canadian stamps and Annabel has 8.
How many Canadian stamps are there altogether?

You could write this as 9 + 8 = 17.

Count up how many New Zealand stamps and how many Australian stamps Ben and Annabel have.

Can you add more than two numbers together?

You don't have to add just two numbers together.
You can add more than two.

On the washing line opposite are 2 socks, 3 T-shirts and 1 tea towel. There are 6 pieces of washing on the line altogether.
The sum that tells the story of this washing line is
2 + 3 + 1 = 6

Look at these washing lines and then look at the sums written at the bottom of the page.

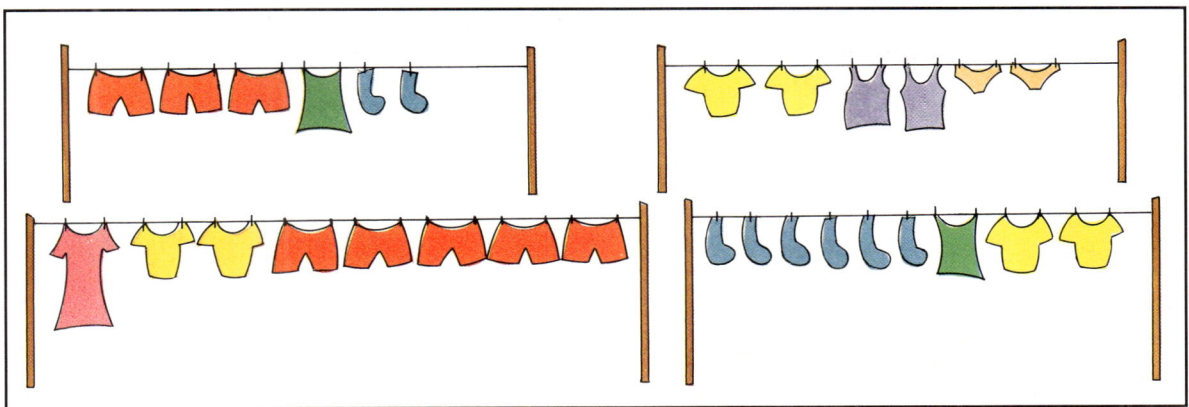

Can you work out which sum is telling the story of which washing line?
1 + 2 + 5 = 8   3 + 1 + 2 = 6   6 + 1 + 2 = 9
2 + 2 + 2 = 6

Can you work out what the sum should be?

Sam has lots of pets. He has 2 budgies, 1 cat, 3 goldfish, 3 mice, 1 parrot and 4 **tropical fish**.

How many of Sam's pets have feathers?
To find this out you need to add together the number of budgies and the number of parrots.
What sum would you write?
What is the answer?

Can you think of sums to find the answers to these questions?
How many of Sam's pets can swim?
How many of his pets have 4 legs?

Glossary

Stall A table or stand where goods which are for sale are displayed.

Symbols Objects or signs which stand for words.

Tag A label which is attached to something.

Tropical fish Fish that are kept at a certain temperature in tanks, which is the same as the temperature of the sea from which they come.

Books To Read

First Book of Numbers, by Angela Wilkes and Claudia Zeff (Usborne, 1982)

Going Places Maths, Leslie Foster (Macdonald, 1985)

How Many?, Fiona Pragoff (Gollancz, 1986)

Introduction to Maths, Nigel Langdon and Janet Cook (Usborne, 1984)

Starting to Add, By Karen Bryant-Mole and Jenny Tyler (Usborne, 1989)

Acknowledgements
Zul Mukhida/Chapel Studios 4, 9, 10, 14, 24, 25; Timothy Woodcock 6, 8, 12, 16, 18, 20, 22, 26, 28. All artwork is by John Yates.

Index

Adding 10, 11, 13, 15, 17, 19, 24, 26, 27
Animals 29

Balloons 19, 21
Books 15

Cars 9, 23
Counting 5, 6, 9, 13, 22, 23

Flowers 13

Marbles 9

Numbers 4, 6, 15, 19, 26

Shells 13
Stall 17
Stamps 25
Sums 14, 15, 16, 17, 19, 21
Symbols 15